MUSTANG

FORD'S WILD PONY

by
LINDA CRAVEN
and
JERRY CRAVEN

THE ROURKE CORPORATION, INC.
Vero Beach, FL 32964

ACKNOWLEDGMENTS

We are grateful to Ford Motor Company for supplying the photographs for this book. Special thanks to Carla Banks and Sandra Nicholls for their invaluable assistance. We are also grateful to Tom Hawthorne for his help with understanding the Mustang, and for allowing us to use the photographs of his Shelby.

© 1993 The Rourke Corporation, Inc.

Library of Congress Cataloging-in-Publication Data
Craven, Linda.
     Mustang: Ford's wild pony / by Linda Craven and Jerry Craven.
         p. cm. – (Car classics)
     Includes index.
     Summary: Gives a brief history of the Mustang automobile and describes its special features and classic models.
     ISBN 0-86593-255-7
     1. Mustang automobile – History – Juvenile literature.
[1. Mustang automobile.] I. Craven, Jerry. II. Title.
III. Series: Car classics (Vero Beach, Fla.)
TL215.M873 1993
629.222'2 – dc20   93-20243
                                         CIP
                                         AC

Printed in the USA

CONTENTS

CHAPTER 1

A CAR FOR THE ADVENTURESOME AMERICAN

The original immigrants who sailed to the New World were adventuresome people. So were those who have immigrated here since, become citizens and had families – the grandparents and great-grandparents of all Americans. The United States is, in fact, a land of adventuresome people on the move.

It's no wonder, then, that a spunky car designed to move fast and look sharp at a reasonable price became an instant American success.

Some refer to the early Mustangs, such as this red convertible, as 1964½ models. Others say they are early 1965 models.

Mustang GT 2-Door Hatchback

Mustang GT Convertible

Mustang LX 5.0L Hatchback

Mustang LX 5.0L Convertible

Mustang LX 5.0L 2-Door Sedan

Mustang LX 2-Door Hatchback

Mustang LX Convertible

Mustang LX 2-Door Sedan

Because Ford sees Americans as lovers of adventure and variety, it offers a wide selection – 10 types – of Mustangs.

The mustang, a wild horse of the North American plains, runs fast and free with mane and tail flying. It seems a natural choice for the name of a sporty car.

However, Ford Motor Company officials considered the names of some other animals before deciding on Mustang. These names included Special Falcon, T-Bird II and Thunderbird II.

John Conley of Ford's ad agency, was a man who liked horses. He suggested a series of Ford cars named for horses, including Colt, Bronco, Pinto and Maverick. To him, "Mustang" had just the right ring of wildness and excitement for Ford's sporty new baby. So Mustang it became.

Lee Iacocca, an executive at Ford Motor Company, wanted Ford automobiles to compete with the European sports cars. However, he also wanted to attract more people than just the racing buffs. He wanted a stylish car that appealed to young people, women and families, as well as to sports car lovers. With its many options, Mustang fit the bill.

CHAPTER 2

A POPULAR PONY

Mustang is one of the most popular cars ever built in America. Confident that it would sell well, Ford Motor Company officials predicted that 100,000 would sell in the first year. In fact, that number sold in just four months!

Mustang was officially presented to the public on April 17, 1964. Less than two years later, in March, 1966, the millionth Mustang rolled off the assembly line.

This early Mustang convertible was made between April and August of 1964.

This ad appeared in June, 1964, in a magazine that published over 7 million copies.

Ford's market researchers carefully studied car buyers. "What kind of car," they asked, "would large numbers of people buy?" Their findings prompted the development of a small, fast car that would appeal to many Americans. So Ford designers went to work on the Mustang.

- The sporty image appealed to sports car enthusiasts.
- Young drivers liked the four-on-the-floor option and bucket seats.
- Women liked the stylish lines and spiffy interior, particularly the convertibles.
- The wide range of options allowed most drivers to choose a combination that pleased.
- Finally, the price, starting at $2,320.86, was affordable for most.

Ford used an advertising blitz for Mustang. Ads appeared everywhere – on television, radio and billboards, in magazines, and newspapers. The big ad campaign, combined with the appeal of the sporty new Mustang, got dramatic results. There are tales of hometown Ford dealers who were overrun by crowds of people eager to see and test drive the new pony in town.

Today Mustangs come with four options of wheels or hubcaps.

CHAPTER 3

THE FIRST PONY

Car makers generally experiment with several designs before selecting one to build and sell to the public. The first Mustang design to reach the eye of anyone outside Ford Motor Company was a low, sleek little model ahead of its time. Engineer Herb Misch and styling chief Eugene Bordinat created a prototype that was driven at the U.S. Grand Prix at Watkins Glen, New York in October, 1962.

Racing buffs loved the car. But Ford executive Lee Iacocca sent designers back to the drawing board. He wanted a car that would appeal to more than just racing enthusiasts.

The basic Mustang shape that eventually went into production was styled by the Ford Division studio, under the guidance of Joe Oros, Gail Halderman and L. David Ash. It was the Oros design that was ultimately approved for production.

This is the interior of a modern Mustang. Red has always been a favorite color among Mustang owners.

1965   1966   1967

1968   1969   1970

1971   1972   1973

Mustang: 1965-1973

The official unveiling of Ford's new design was April 17, 1964. However, there were several well-planned "leaks" prior to that date. For example, Henry Ford's 20-year-old nephew drove a black Mustang convertible to a luncheon prior to the official unveiling. *Newsweek* magazine and others ran the story and photos.

On the evening of April 16, Ford purchased prime-time slots on all three major television networks. Thus, 27 million Americans were given a preview of Ford's flashy new baby.

CHAPTER 4

A MID-YEAR DEBUT

This is one of the now highly-prized 1964½ Mustang convertibles.

Ford designers had originally worked on a small, two-seater model sports car. But Ford executive Lee Iacocca insisted a four-seater would sell better. Automotive sales history proves he was right. The four-seater Mustang has been one of the best sellers of the American auto industry.

Most new model cars come out in the fall of the prior year. For example, 1994 model cars appeared on the dealers' lots in the fall of 1993. However, Mustang first appeared in the spring of 1964, not in the fall. Ford called these first models early 1965s. But some people have called them 1964½ models. Mustangs built after August 17, 1964, are commonly called late '65s.

Experts say there are some differences between the early '65s (those built before August 17) and the late '65s. For example, the early '65s came with generators, while the late '65s had alternators. The early cars also had a stationary passenger seat, a smaller handle on the automatic transmission shift, and larger horns. There were additional differences in the engines.

A 2 X 2 fastback body style was introduced in September, 1964. From March, 1965, a luxury interior was available. It had embossed ponies on the seats. The letter "B" appeared on the body code of the warranty plates of those that had the embossed seats.

This is a late 1965 Mustang.

The 1966 Mustang looked almost identical to the 1965 model.

CHAPTER 5

BIGGER, BETTER, AND THE COBRA JET

The Mustang was so popular in 1965-66 that other car makers decided to offer competing models. General Motors, which makes Chevrolet, came out with the Camaro. Chrysler and American Motors produced the Javelin. So Ford designers and engineers scrambled to make the 1967-68 Mustangs better than ever.

The first change was to make them bigger. The 1967 was wider, longer, higher and heavier than before. It also had a bigger engine, and a number of new options were available. The Mustang GT equipment included:

- power disc front brakes
- stiffer springs
- adjustable shock absorbers
- 15-inch steel wheels, with imitation wire wheel covers
- quicker-ratio steering
- wider tires (F70 X 14)
- dual exhausts with quad outlets.

The 1967 Mustang was longer and heavier than the earlier models.

New interior options were also added. Some of the new features included:

- tilt-away steering wheel
- fold-down rear seat (fastback only)
- cruise control.

Other design features available on the 1967-68 Mustangs were a glass rear window for convertibles, wheel well moldings, and a louvered hood that held turn signal lights.

Ford unveiled the 428 Cobra Jet on April Fools' Day, 1968. This get-up-and-go engine had an additional cubic inch of engine displacement. The 428 CJ delivered a lot of power through its four-speed gear box. Other new design features were the ram air scoop and staggered shock absorbers (with the four-speed manual model).

The 1967 fastback model was popular with Mustang lovers and has remained a favorite among enthusiasts.

The 1967 Mustang may have grown in size and weight, but it kept its reputation as a sporty, fun car.

CHAPTER 6

THE BOSS AND MACH I

This 1969 Mach I has retaining pins with cables attached to the front.

Two men had great influence on the new direction Mustang took in 1969-70. They were Semon E. "Bunkie" Knudsen, who left General Motors to become Ford president in 1968. The other was styling specialist Larry Shinoda, who had worked on the GM Corvette.

One of Shinoda's first moves was to come up with a new name for a newly designed 1969 model: the Boss. The car was made almost an inch wider and nearly 2 inches longer than the 1968 model, although the 108-inch wheelbase remained the same. The body was also an inch and a half lower, and the car weighed about 175 pounds more. In appearance, the sculptured side scoop was softened. One pair of headlights was inside the grille, the other recessed to the outside.

Engine options included the Boss 302, the 428 Super Cobra Jet Ram Air, and the Boss 429. The big-block 429 V-8 was popular as a drag racer, though many used it as a street car. At $4,798 it was the most expensive Boss. Only 852 were sold in 1968.

The 1969 Mach I was fitted with special features, such as a hood painted in flat black anti-glare paint similar to that on professional racers. It also had a fake air scoop, optional racing-style hood retaining pins, reflective side and tail stripes, a chrome pop-open gas cap, and body-colored racing mirrors.

In 1969-70 there were 10 engines available, two 6-cylinder and eight V-8s ranging in horsepower from 115 to 375.

The 1970 Boss 302 was built low and powerful.

CHAPTER 7

THE SHELBY HOT RODS

Carroll Shelby was a successful race car driver turned designer. He had little interest in building a car that would appeal to a lot of people and sell in large numbers. Instead, he wanted to create a car suited to the few dedicated hot-rod lovers in the country – a car that would leap forward and stay ahead of the pack.

He succeeded. Race enthusiasts loved the Shelby Mustangs from the beginning. "The Shelby was fast and fun to drive," said one owner. "It had the power and the feel of a champion sports car, not of a car made for taking grocery shopping."

This 1968 Shelby GT 500 has the Cobra logo on the side just behind the front wheel.

The 1965 Shelby GT 350R	
Length	181.6 inches
Width	68.2 inches
Height	51 inches
Weight	2,600 pounds
Wheelbase	108 inches
Track	Front, 56 inches
	Rear, 56 inches
Weight Distribution	57 front/43 rear
Engine	Rated 350 bhp
Swept Volume	289 cubic inches
Bore	4 inches
Stroke	2.87 inches
Compression Ratio	10.5:1
Performance	0-60 mph in about 6 seconds
Standing Quarter	13 seconds
Top Speed	About 140 mph

This 1978 Mustang King Cobra featured a T-bar roof.

The Shelby Mustang was not built for comfort. It was not intended for driving to work and back, nor for traveling long distances. The clutch was stiff. There were no power brakes or steering, so braking was tight and parking hard. The car was also noisy – which pleased the car owners but displeased their neighbors.

While most of the distinctive features of the Shelby Mustangs were under the hood, Ford wanted to make the special hot cars visibly recognizable. Side stripes were used on many GT 350s. And a bold front-to-rear stripe, straight over the top of the car, became a popular mark.

The Mustang emblem appeared only on the gas cap and on the right side of the grille on all Shelbys.

CHAPTER 8

THE COLLECTIBLE SHELBYS

The Shelby Mustang was a purist's or enthusiast's racing car. It has since become a hot item among car collectors. Only 562 GT 350s were built in 1965; 37 of them were the GT 350R – the racing version. In 1966, 2,380 Shelbys were sold. Curiously enough, 1,000 of them were purchased by the Hertz Rent A Car company.

Shelby Mustangs were made and sold only during the years 1965 to 1970. Today, all of them that remain are collector's items – like rare coins or stamps.

The 306 brake horsepower (bhp) engine was the base unit in the 1967 Shelby. Two bigger engines were available: (1) the 428 cubic inch displacement (cid) V-8 engine rated at 355 bhp, and (2) the 427 with 425 bhp. The 47 Mustangs in which the 427 engines were used were called GT 500s, and they were the most powerful Mustangs ever built.

During the 1968 model year, the GT 500 was replaced by the GT 500KR (King of the Road), with an engine rated at 355 bhp. Because Ford ran short of the big 428 engines in 1968, they substituted the smaller engine on some cars, at a loss of about 75 bhp.

1970 was the last year Ford sold Shelby Mustangs. However, in 1980-82, designer Carroll Shelby took some used 1966 convertibles and built a dozen 1966-specification Shelby Mustang convertibles. Some purists say they are not the real thing. However, few say they would refuse to own one if given the chance.

This illustration appears on a brochure of The Mustang Club of America. Placing a drawing of a Shelby in the center shows how important the model is to lovers of classic Mustangs.

Shelbys had few Mustang logos on them, but modern Mustangs display them many places, including in the center of the optional aluminum wheels.

This is a classic 1968 Mustang GT Fastback Shelby Cobra.

CHAPTER 9

MUSTANG II

In the early 1970s, almost all American cars were large and heavy. Even the Mustangs of this era were larger and heavier than their earlier brothers.

Lee Iacocca believed it was time to again produce a small, sporty version. For the 1974 model year he held an in-house competition, challenging designers to see who could come up with the best Mustang design.

The design that won was a smaller, sleeker vehicle. And the timing couldn't have been better. The new Mustang came out just as an oil and gas shortage hit the world. With gasoline prices soaring, American drivers wanted a more efficient machine. Mustang fit the bill.

The 1974 model was shorter by over half a yard than the 1973. At 175 inches, it was 6.6 inches shorter even than the original Mustang. Its wheelbase also dropped – from 109 inches to 96.2. The 1974 model was also almost 4 inches narrower than the 1973, but it was still nearly 2 inches wider than the original model.

America's first all-metric engine appeared on the 1974 4-cylinder model Mustang. A V-6 engine was also an option. Rack and pinion steering was superior to the older recirculating ball type. Disc brakes on the front were standard equipment.

In terms of body style options, buyers could choose the hardtop coupe or a fastback design.

The 1974 Mustang	
Length	175 inches
Width	70.2 inches
Height	50.3 inches
Weight	2,700 pounds
Wheelbase	96.2 inches
Track	Front, 55.6 inches
	Rear, 55.8 inches
Weight Distribution	59 front/41 rear
Engine	Rated 88 bhp
Bore	3.78 inches
Stroke	3.126 inches
Compression Ratio	8.4:1
Performance	0-60 mph in about 15 seconds
Standing Quarter	Around 20 seconds
Top Speed	Just over 100 mph

The 1978 Mustang II offered an optional sunroof.

*Ford downsized
its pony with the 1974 Mustang II.*

This is a 1976 Mach I fastback.

CHAPTER 10

PACE CARS AND NEW CONVERTIBLES

In 1979 the new Mustang was chosen as the Pace Car for the Indianapolis 500 race. The Pace Cars actually used in the race were fitted with hopped-up 302 cubic inch displacement – 5.0 liter – engines. About 11,000 Pace Car replicas were made to sell to the public. Pace Car buyers could choose the hot 302 cid V-8 engine or the turbo four.

The body design of the Pace Car included the T-top convertible. It had removable panels on either side of a center bar that ran from front to back. The T-top gave better crash protection than a true convertible.

For 10 years no Mustang convertibles were built (except the T-top models). In 1983 Ford reintroduced the classic convertible. It was instantly popular. With a standard 5-speed gear box, it had a power roof and a glass rear window.

This 1983 GT Hardtop gave Mustang a more modern appearance.

The top folds into a smaller space on more recent Mustang convertibles.

After a 10-year absence, the Mustang convertible reappeared in 1983.

Ford celebrated the 20th anniversary of Mustangs in 1984 with a special model. All anniversary models were painted white with red interiors. A special anniversary badge was mounted on the dash. A second badge with the buyer's name engraved on it was mailed to the owner after purchase.

The late 1980s and early 1990s Mustangs had much in common with the earliest models. The newer models are quieter, smoother and faster, but they retain their reputation as a fun, sporty, car-lover's car.

CHAPTER 11

THE MUSTANG CLUB OF AMERICA

Few cars have inspired the kind of loyalty found among Mustang lovers. They like to get together to share their enthusiasm, to show one another their cars and to socialize. To help them in their goals, they have formed The Mustang Club of America.

It is the largest and most active car club in America. Since it began in 1976, almost 28,000 people have joined. The number of active members is around 7,000. The club, called MCA by the members, holds national shows and sponsors regional shows all over the country. The MCA sets rules for judging Mustangs in competition.

The rules are based on the "purity" of the cars. To get high scores in competition, a car must have equipment, body parts and paint that meet the factory specifications when the car was new. If a 1966 Mustang came off the assembly line as a white car, that information will be encoded in the car's serial number. The owner who shows the car will lose points in an MCA contest if the car is any other color.

MCA also publishes a monthly magazine of club news. The magazine contains advertisements for suppliers of MCA-approved Mustang parts. A club member pays $25 in annual dues. For that fee, the family members are also considered members.

Local chapters often have family picnics, and many get together for special holiday parties, such as Easter egg hunts.

  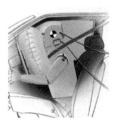 

Today's Mustangs come equipped with many safety features including an air bag.

This is the logo of the MCA. Members can buy hats, t-shirts, bumper stickers and many other items with this logo on it.

February	Mustang Owners Club of California	Van Nuys, CA
March	The Gulf Coast Regional Mustang Club	Pensacola, FL
April	Anniversary of introduction of Mustang	Detroit, MI
May	The Central Arkansas Mustang Club	Little Rock, AR
June	The Tri-State Mustang Club	Cincinnati, OH
July	The Shiloh Valley Mustang Club	Belleville, IL
September	The Foothills Mustang Club	Greenville, SC
October	The Tennessee Valley Mustang Club	Oak Ridge, TN

This is a typical calendar of Mustang shows for a year, as announced by Mustang Times. *This list does not include numerous smaller meets and shows hosted by MCA groups across America.*

CHAPTER 12

REBUILDING A CLASSIC CAR

Car lovers so value the Shelby Mustang that seldom is one scrapped, no matter how damaged it might be.

Consider the case of Tom Hawthorne. His home and garage went up in flames, burning his 1966 Shelby almost beyond recognition. Tom made no attempt to rebuild the destroyed house, but he did rebuild the Shelby. And if he had not done so, he could easily have sold the burned hulk to someone who would.

"It cost me about $45,000 to remake the car," Tom said. "But when I finished the job, it was worth about $100,000."

The fire reduced the interior of the car to a wheelbarrow full of ash, and it burned out all the wiring of the electrical system.

A fire destroyed the interior and rippled the body panels on this 1966 Shelby, making rebuilding a challenge.

To qualify for car shows, all replacement parts had to fit original factory specifications.

Tom put the burned Shelby on a gigantic rotisserie so he could turn it during the process of repairing the fire damage. He had to replace everything except the frame and the engine.

"Basically, what I have now," Tom said, "is a handmade car. It still has the original Shelby numbers stamped on the engine and under the fender, so it qualifies in car shows as an original Shelby."

Even the original color, as indicated by a code on the engine, had to be restored to make the Shelby qualify as authentic.

The once-destroyed Shelby has won trophies at several car shows. Any lover of Mustangs would look at Tom Hawthorne's slick, red Shelby and agree that rebuilding was worth the effort.

CHAPTER 13

THE STATE-OF-THE-ART MUSTANG

Ford Motor Company likes to point out the latest Mustang's flashy and comfortable interior. The driver gets treated to comfortable seats, a leather-covered steering wheel, a great sound system (with a CD player option), tinted glass, variable speed wipers and so on.

A sports car purist might complain that the Mustang falls short of being a classic sports car. Still, the latest Mustang looks and handles enough like a sports car to have a wide appeal, especially among those who value comfortable driving.

The 1993 Mustang offers 225 horsepower at 4200 rpm in a 5.0 liter V-8 engine. The engine's torque, or driving power, is an impressive 300 pound feet at 3200 rpm. It is equipped with a sophisticated sequential electronic fuel injection system that directs fuel to the cylinders to match exactly the firing order from spark plugs. There are two spark plugs per cylinder.

Drivers like the road-handling capabilities as well as the sporty lines of the 1993 Mustang.

Fuel injection and other engine functions are controlled by computer. When the driver meets slick road conditions, the traction-lok rear axle shifts torque to the rear wheel with most traction.

The 1993 model comes with a five-on-the-floor stick shift or an optional automatic transmission. Two of the 1993 models – the GT and LX 5.0L – have as standard equipment five-spoke aluminum wheels.

For the future, Ford will produce Mustangs with classic Mustang appeal. These will be cars with a sporty look and smooth handling at relatively low cost.

The interior of the contemporary Mustang is a study in comfort and beauty.

CHAPTER 14

MUSTANG: IMPORTANT DATES

1964 The first Mustangs appear. Those built between March and August 17 are called 1964½ or early 1965 models. Least expensive sticker price was $2,329.96.

1965-70 Shelby Mustangs were made (562 in 1965; 2,830 in 1966; 3,225 in 1967; 4,450 in 1968; 3,153 in 1969-70).

1967 Mustang was redesigned, making it longer and wider though still on a 108-inch wheelbase. A V-8 engine option was added. It had a 390 cid and produced 320 hp.

1969 The second major restyling was introduced; Ford produced the Boss; there were ten engine options, from a 6-cylinder 115 hp to a V-8 with 375 hp. The least expensive Mustang was $2,618.

1971 Ford produced the largest, heaviest Mustang yet. It had a 109-inch wheelbase. The least expensive Mustang: $2,911.

1973 Ford made the last factory-built convertible Mustang for 10 years; the next one appeared in 1983.

1974 Mustang II appeared and was called "the second generation." Wheelbase shrank to 96.2 inches, and a 4-cylinder engine was introduced. The V-8 was dropped; only two engines were available. The larger was a V-6, 171 cubic inch with 105 hp. The least expensive Mustang: $3,134.

1975 The V-8 engine returns; it was a 302 cubic inch with 140 hp.

1976 The last year engine displacement was measured in cubic inches; for later models, Ford measures engine displacement in liters.

1979 The third major redesign was introduced. The wheelbase increased to 100.4 inches. There were five engine options: a 4-cylinder, two 6-cylinder options, and two versions of the V-8. The least expensive Mustang: $4,494.

1983 The Mustang convertible was reintroduced. The least expensive Mustang: $6,727.

1988 The front and back of the Mustang became more rounded. Two engines were available: a 4-cylinder, 2.3 liter 88 hp; and a V-8 5 liter 225 hp. The least expensive Mustang: $8,271.

1990 Mustang came out with a driver's-side air bag. The least expensive Mustang: $9,753.

1993 The two engines available were a 4-cylinder, 2.3 liter with 105 hp, and a V-8 5 liter with 205 hp.

Current and Future Mustangs:

Ford increasingly emphasizes design that maximizes driver and passenger safety; computer technology will continue to be built into Mustangs for greater efficiency and performance.

GLOSSARY

1964½ model – The first Mustangs, specifically those made between March and August 17 of 1964.

air scoop – An opening in a car body for drawing in air, usually for cooling brakes or engine; the early Mustangs had fake air scoops on the sides in front of the rear wheels.

alternator – A device for recharging the battery.

bhp – Brake horsepower; a measurement of engine power by using a braking device to determine the amount of power an engine has at high revolutions per minute (rpm).

Boss – The name given to a model of Mustang, first made in 1969.

cid – Cubic inch displacement.

CJ – Initials used to refer to the Cobra Jet, a powerful Mustang first made in 1968.

four-on-the-floor – A 4-speed manual transmission with the gear shift on the floorboard.

generator – A device for recharging the battery found in the early 1964½ Mustangs; alternators replaced generators.

GT – Initials standing for "Grand Touring," used on Mustang and many other cars.

MCA – The Mustang Club of America.

pace car – The car that drives in front of race cars on the track; the pace car sets the pace (often in excess of 100 mph) while keeping the racers in starting order, then it gets out of the way for the race to begin.

prototype – An original form that serves as a model on which later models are based.

quad outlets – The four places exhaust is vented from some models of Mustangs.

rpm – Revolutions per minute.

Shelby Mustangs – Specially-built Mustangs designed for racing by Carroll Shelby; these were made by Ford Motor Company from 1965 to 1970.

standing quarter – Refers to the fastest time a car can travel one-quarter of a mile from a dead stop.

T-top – A car with a T-bar roof structure; a T-top is almost a convertible, but offers more driver protection should the car roll.

torque – Turning force, a measure of engine power at low rpm.

traction-lok – The device on modern Mustangs that shifts power to the wheel with most traction when the car hits slick spots on the road.

This is the Mustang 5.0 liter V-8 engine. HO stands for "high output.

INDEX